The Silvertoı

Mary Ann Olsen

Alpha Editions

This edition published in 2023

ISBN : 9789357938952

Design and Setting By
Alpha Editions
www.alphaedis.com
Email - info@alphaedis.com

The Silverton Story

Silverton, Looking South Toward Durango

Silverton, with all its scenic splendor, nestles in a valley 9,302 feet in altitude. It is surrounded by four mountain peaks, all of which rise above timberline, and are usually snow covered the year around; Kendall Mountain to the East, Anvil Mountain to the West, Boulder Mountain to the North, and Sultan Mountain to the South. The highest of these peaks is Sultan, which rises to a dizzy height of 13,336 feet. Opposite this is Kendall that juts skyward 4,000 feet above the floor of the valley. Silverton is centered in the rugged, majestic San Juan Mountains, and nowhere in the nation is there another 100,000 square miles of such spectacularly scenic grandeur.

One evening, a group of men were in a saloon discussing the possibilities of the San Juan. One fellow remarked, "We have silver by the ton", and thus Silverton got its name. It is the only incorporated town in the county, and boasts not an acre of farm land.

Silverton was, at one time, named Baker's Park after Charles Baker who led a group of prospectors to this country in 1860 or 1861. There is no record of any permanent locations made, or of any quantity of mineral taken out, though there were indications of prospecting being done. As you can imagine, Baker and his party endured many hardships. Relics, broken wagon parts, and some discarded camp equipment lead to the belief the party came by way of Durango, thence to Cascade Creek along the route of our present highway. From there they went to the West of Spud Mountain and kept fairly high, crossing Coal Bank Hill and following around the head of Lime Creek. After passing Lime Creek, they crossed the hills East of there and came down into the park by way of Bear Creek. There is a place on Bear Creek which shows they let their wagons down the hillside by means of a rope, as the stock was evidently unable to hold the wagons under control.

Charles Baker had a narrow escape in 1862 near Eureka. One of the men organized a mutiny, crying out to hang Baker, claiming he had deceived them. Baker heard of it and escaped, otherwise he would have met his fate at the hands of his own men. In 1868, Baker again set out from Denver for Silverton, as he still believed gold was here, and arrived in the San Juan in 1871. He was killed in this vicinity by the Indians shortly thereafter.

Dempsey Reese, Miles T. Johnson, Adam French and Thomas Blair outfitted in Santa Fe and arrived in the San Juans in 1870. They were the first lode prospectors, as Baker and his party had been searching for placer gold.

No one wintered in Silverton during the years 1870-'71-'72. Dempsey Reese and his party, accompanied by William Mulholand and Francis M. Snowden, came back the following spring, and this was the first record of any permanent discovery, namely, the "Little Giant Gold Mine", located in Arastra Gulch. The lode produced ore of such quantity and value as to warrant its being packed on burros to Pueblo for processing. Samples of the ore showed from 400 to 900 ounces of gold per ton. This rich ledge, which was treated by arastras, was without a doubt the beginning of the future of the San Juans. The first quartz mill for the reduction of ore was built in 1873 for the use of the Little Giant Mine.

There were about forty or fifty prospectors in the county by this time, but the year 1873 was a banner year for mining claims. More than three thousand claims were recorded, and the population grew by several hundred. Many of the large producers were located in that year and in 1872. Notably the Sunnyside, Shenandoah, Silver Lake and portions of the Gold King Group. Some of the Shenandoah claims have produced ore in considerable quantities each year since 1875.

Within months after being married, Mr. Stoiber of Silver Lake Mine fame, became one of the richest men in the state of Colorado. Two of Mrs. Stoiber's claims to fame were having four husbands, and building the huge Stoiberhof Mansion in Denver and the Silver Lake Mansion in Silverton. At her first home in Silverton, Mrs. Stoiber had an argument with her neighbor, so she eliminated him from her consciousness by building a towering wall around her property which completely cut off her view of him. Apparently this action struck her fancy, for she was to repeat it. When Mr. Stoiber sold his mining interests to the Guggenheim family for a reported two and a half million dollars, he built the biggest, gaudiest, and most lavish house in Denver. "Stoiberhof" was completed in 1906, and was filled with the most fabulous collection of objets d'art Denver had ever seen. Again in Denver Mrs. Stoiber argued with the owner of the adjoining property, and again she built a wall twelve feet high around her grounds. Egbert W. Reed, the owner, armed himself with a court order, and for months the affair dragged through the courts. Mrs. Lena Allen Webster Stoiber Rood Ellis died in Italy in March, 1935. Few remember her, or the fact that her first fortune came from the Silverton area.

San Juan County, in its entirety, was included in the grant to the Ute Indians in 1868. Three years later, when mining began to boom, the Indians protested against the whites coming into their territory. In 1872, troops were sent out by the government to keep the miners off this grant and in February, 1873, an order was issued by the Department of the Interior warning all miners to vacate by June 1st. The troops had proceeded up the Rio Grande a considerable distance when the order was suspended by the President, and a new treaty was made with the Indians, which was effected by paying Chief Ouray $1,000.00. The Utes surrendered some three million acres of land.

In July, 1873, while the Brunot Treaty was pending between the Ute Indians and the United States Government for the lands of the reservation, when the great excitement over the rich and extensive mining broke out, Mr. Tower made arrangements with Jackson Foundry and the George Trick Hardware Company of Denver for the materials to erect a sawmill. This was shipped by the D. & R. G. Railroad to Colorado Springs. There a contract was made with the freighters to deliver this to Silverton. The charges were sixteen cents per pound. The journey to Del Norte was a pleasant one, but then the trouble began. From the South Fork of the Rio Grande River, sixteen miles above Del Norte to the head waters of the stream, they forded the river fifty-seven times. The outfit consisted of three teams, ten persons and 6,000 pounds of freight. Only the old pioneers of the area can fully understand the trouble, dangers and hardships encountered in working freight over the mountains in those days. Two weeks after leaving Del Norte, they arrived at the present site of Howardsville. Aided by a number of miners they were able, after a week of hard work, to get the wagons to Silverton. A location was made for the mill on Mineral Creek at the foot of Sultan Mountain, and here Mr. Tower erected the first sawmill. Mrs. Tower, a bride of nineteen from Chicago, accompanied the party and returned in the fall to Del Norte. Thus, Mrs. Tower was the first white woman in Silverton.

Chief Ouray and Otto Mears

The first mercantile establishment in the county was a combined saloon and general merchandise store located at Howardsville. This was in 1874, and the post office at Howardsville was opened that same fall with W. H. Nichols as postmaster. Mrs. Nichols, Mrs. W. E. Earl, Mrs. John F. Cotton, and Mrs. H. F. Tower were among the first women in the county. Mrs. Merril Doud came a few weeks later.

When the population of southern Colorado had grown to such an extent that a Courthouse was necessary, Howardsville was the center of population and therefore the logical site for the county seat of La Plata County. A small log building was erected and served the entire western slope from the northern to the southern boundary and from the San Luis Valley to the western line of the state. In the summer of this year the county seat was moved from Howardsville to Silverton. The first store in town was called Greene and Company, and Francis M. Snowden built the first cabin. It was located where the hospital now stands on the avenue that bears his name, and was the social gathering place of the town. All the noted personages who visited in the early days stopped here, and if the "Colonel," as he was known, had kept a register it would be an interesting document today. Dances were held there, with John and Armanda Cotton furnishing the music.

The County's First Courthouse, Located at Howardsville, Now Destroyed
by Fire

Also in 1874 a preliminary survey of the township was made by Thomas
Trip and a complete survey was made that same year by William Monroe
and J. M. Hanks. As the streets came into being, they were given names of
the prominent pioneers of the 70's—Greene, Reese, Snowden, Blair, etc.
The following year was a busy one. The first white child in Silverton was
born to Mr. and Mrs. Ben Harwood. The child was named Frank, and
lived here his entire life. Ben Harwood was quite a noted character in the
early life of the San Juans. He was without a doubt a very strong and
untiring man. It is an authenticated fact that for several winters he packed
the mail on snowshoes from Watson's Cabin, at the foot of Grassy Hill,
to Howardsville and Silverton, at the same time carrying from fifty to
sixty pounds of beef on his back for the Highland Mary Mine.

Francis M. Snowden in Front of His Cabin—The First Cabin in Silverton

The La Plata Miner was the first newspaper, with John R. Curry of Iowa as editor and owner. Several years later the name was changed to the Silverton Miner, and since 1920 it has been called the Silverton Standard and the Miner. From 1874 it has never missed an issue. Still to be seen at the Standard office is the old 1830 Model Hoe original press which was used continually until a short time ago.

A road, barely passable, from Watson's Cabin at Grassy Hill to Howardsville and Silverton by way of Stony Pass was completed. The grade from the cabin to timberline on this side of the pass was fairly good, but just below the timberline was a short, steep pitch which often defied the brakes. Freighters would cut a fair sized spruce tree and tie it on behind their wagons as a holdback over this pitch.

Silverton Standard Office, Taken in 1955, with D. & R. G. Conductor
Myron Henry

When trees were no longer available, Squire (W. D.) Watson selected a solid stump at the top of the incline, and lowered the wagons by means of a snubbing rope. The price was $2.50 for about two-hundred feet, which made it pretty profitable. The summer travel was from five to twenty wagons daily. The freight rate at this time from Del Norte to Silverton was 30 dollars a ton, and remained so until the coming of the railroad.

The first United States District Court was held in Silverton, with Judge Hallett presiding. It seems the same faces were appearing in the jury box, and the reason was the benches were so splintery they had to choose men who wore leather seats in their trousers.

President Grant appointed J. M. Hanks as the first postmaster. For several weeks after the appointment, he could find no building suitable for a postoffice and carried the mail in his pockets and handed it out on the streets when he saw any of the addressees. Mail services were few and far between in the winter of 1875 and '76. Twice, Big Alec Fleming brought in on his back a load of mail from Del Norte, wearing snow shoes or skis nearly every foot of the way.

Our first school was started this year. When the town was laid out, a lot on the corner of Snowden Avenue and Eleventh Street had been set aside for school purposes. The school served as a church or for any public gathering, and was a low, log building. In 1887 the school record states they had six visitors and 144 cases of tardiness. In 1879, the census showed forty pupils between the ages of six and twenty-one, and by 1890, the total school attendance was 153.

The start of the Durango-Silverton road was made in 1875. A crude mountain road reached from the present site of Rockwood for about sixteen miles to the top of Coal Bank Hill. Here the road ceased and the Old Ute Trail was used by pack animals for the remaining fourteen miles into Silverton. The old trail was used until about 1877 or '78 when a prospector, with the help of others, built a toll road up the Animas Canyon. The road started north of Rockwood, crossed the site of what is now Lake Electra, then made a drop of 2,000 feet in a distance of one and a half miles to the bottom of the canyon. Here it crossed Cascade Creek at its junction with the Animas and continued up the river to Silverton, making many crossings along the way. A toll gate was located at the entrance to the canyon near the Champion Mine. There was also a toll gate at Baker's Bridge below Rockwood, and the fee was $3.00. Many parts of the old road can still be seen from the train.

State Highway Approaching Silverton from Durango to the South.
Approximate Site of the Old Toll Gate

Otto Mears, known as the Pathfinder of the San Juan, laid out a system of toll roads through the San Juans, branching in all directions from Silverton—up the river to Eureka and Animas Forks, over the Ophir Range, down the San Miguel River to the Dallas, across to Telluride and again across to Rico and Rockwood, and from Silverton to Ouray—four hundred miles, mostly toll. Like networks these roads were, and are, of untold benefits. In 1875 Mears was paid the grand sum of $600.00 for building a road up the Animas River from Silverton to Howardsville,

Eureka, Animas Forks, and Mineral Point, apportioned as follows: Silverton to Howardsville, $150.00; Howardsville to Eureka, $150.00; and from Eureka to Mineral Point, $300.00.

La Plata County was cut off from San Juan County in 1876, and Silverton was incorporated. At that time the town was said to have around 500 voters. The first meeting of the council was held, and among the board members was F. M. Snowden. After the division of San Juan and La Plata counties, our county was still of considerable size and in January, 1877, Ouray, San Miguel, and a portion of Dolores counties were set off, leaving San Juan at its present size.

In 1877, Otto Mears built a road from Animas Forks to Lake City. Most of the ore from Poughkeepsie Gulch, Mineral Point and Animas Forks was treated at Lake City.

One of the oldest Masonic Lodges in the state is the San Juan Lodge No. 33, A. F. & A. M. which was organized in 1877. The organization has had a remarkable life, and is a strong factor in the community.

Congregational Church, Built in 1881

The Congregational Church was organized in 1878. Although faced by many trials and tribulations, and at times by lack of money, the church has managed to survive. The present church building was constructed in 1881 and A. P. Roberts was the pastor from 1878 to 1882.

This same year, Charles Fisher, who built the brewery at Howardsville, moved it to Silverton and ran it for many years in the old stone building on the bank of Mineral Creek at the lower end of the town. He built the

Fisher Building on Greene Street which is the brick building occupied and owned for the past several years by the Maffey family (French Bakery). The building next to Maffey was the livery stables. The wagons and carriages were housed on the ground floor and the horses were taken up a ramp and stabled on the second floor.

The first record of Lynch Law was in August 31 of this year. The following is a report from a newspaper: "About two o'clock in the morning of August 31, 1878 unknown parties entered the jail and took Henry Cleary, charged with the murder of James M. Brown, and hung him on the ox frame in the rear of the blacksmith shop on upper Greene Street."

Silverton had become a town of considerable population by 1879, and fire protection became a necessity. A "hook and ladder" was ordered from Denver, and with news of its arrival at Grassy Hill at the head of the Rio Grande, nearly half of the male population started for Grassy on horseback and on burros. The hook and ladder with all its equipment was hauled to Howardsville where it was met by another group who brought it into Silverton by hand. The Silverton Cornet Band led the group from Howardsville, and that evening a big celebration was held. At the old City Hall on Blair Street, next door to Swanson's Market, you can still see part of the old fire fighting Hose Cart; also two cells of the old county jail remain there.

Patrick, better known as "Cap" Stanley, opened the first brick yard at the foot of the hill between Reese Street and the Walsh Smelter. He built the first two brick homes in Silverton on the east side of upper Greene Street, and they are yet in very good condition. The bricks for the Grand Imperial Hotel were made in this yard. "Cap" was the leader of the Vigilantes, and a bluff, stern person. The Vigilantes did their work well, but at one time the town council, realizing that matters were becoming serious, hired the famous Bat Masterson of Dodge City fame to clean up the town. Needless to say, he did.

Fred Steinger secured a government contract for ten thousand dollars to bring the mail to Silverton from Parrot City. This was known as the Star Route and was a daily schedule with three stops and three changes of horses each trip. Meals and sleeping quarters were provided for the passengers should they desire or be forced to stay. There were log barns at all stops, and care for the horses was provided. It was not an unusual sight to see one hundred to one hundred and fifty pack animals turned out for grazing on the slopes of the hills. All went well during the summer, but winter was not so good. The carriers started in wagons, then later had to leave the wagons and use horses. Finally, when the snow got so deep at the stop below Silverton, a carrier by the name of Snyder would use his dog team and sled. He would pile the mail, general merchandise, and supplies on the sled, then he would perch himself on top of the load and be on his way. The sled was pulled by his huge black dogs that were both strong and savage. Snyder and his dog team also hauled water for the town in winter. He would fill six five-gallon oil cans, put them on the sled, and he and his trusty dogs were off to deliver water at fifty cents a can. The dogs were also utilized at funerals when the snow was too deep for the heavier animals. Snyder took good care of his dogs, and after a hard trip, so the story goes, he would give each of them a drink of whiskey.

In 1879, a fire broke out in the forests near Molas Pass. There are two stories told about the "Molas" or "Lime Creek" burn. One is, the fire was started by a camp fire left burning by careless campers, and the other, which is the most popular, that the Indians had set the forest afire to smoke out the white settlers. There had been trouble between the Utes and the whites, and men at the Animas Forks section, seeing the smoke, thought it was an Indian uprising and hid in the mine for several days. The blaze burned more than 26,000 acres of timberland and consumed an estimated 150 million board feet of timber.

Replanting of the burn began in 1924, and since then about 1,000 trees have been planted annually. Even so, eighty-three years later, the scars remain. Beautiful Molas Lake, owned by the Town of Silverton, is located five miles south and near the summit of Molas Pass. Silverton is surrounded by seven lakes above timberline that teem with native trout. So high are they that stocking is done by airplane.

Molas Lake, with Needle Mountains in the Background

In 1880, Otto Mears had a toll road from Saguache to Silverton, via Poncha Pass, Marshall Pass, Gunnison, Cebolla, Lake Fork, Animas Forks, Eureka and Howardsville, totalling 200 miles, with eight to ten toll stations.

May 28, 1880, Thatcher Brothers of Pueblo opened the Bank of Silverton. In July, 1880, Jefferman and Johnson opened the Bank of San Juan. This bank was sold to the Thatchers in 1882.

In December, 1882, application was made for a charter, and on April 18, 1883, the First National Bank was opened. This bank had only two cashiers in fifty-one years. It was liquidated in 1934, paying one-hundred cents on the dollar. This bank was located on the corner of Greene and 13th Streets, which is now the Recreation Hall.

Thomas Walsh Residence in Animas Forks, as It Looks Today

The year 1881 saw the construction of the Martha Rose Smelter, the slag piles of which still remain at the southwestern edge of the town. A few years later this smelter was purchased by Thomas Walsh who had mined quite extensively in the Animas Forks section. The old Walsh residence still stands in Animas Forks. When Otto Mears built the Silverton Railroad from Silverton to Ironton Park, the smelter treated an average of over fifteen cars of crude ore a day. It was from this smelter that Mr. Walsh obtained the money to purchase the Camp Bird Mine. The production and sale of the Camp Bird brought him over ten million dollars. His daughter, Evelyn Walsh McLean, was once the owner of the famous Hope Diamond. "Cap" Stanley once refereed a prize fight held at the Walsh Smelter and entered the ring as the third man with a gun strapped around his waist. There was no doubt as to the superiority of one of the contestants, but evidently thinking of getting a return bout, which might make him another fifty to a hundred dollars, he made no effort to win. Cap, quickly discerning the trend of things, pulled his gun and ordered the men to fight. A quick knock-out was the result.

Blair Street as You Look Toward Sultan Mountain

The Denver & Rio Grande on "The Highline"

In its heyday, Blair Street reveled around the clock. No less than thirty-two establishments lined its two gay blocks and beckoned from the fringes of the side streets. The gambling houses carried such names as Mikado, National, Diamond, Sage Hen, and Bon Ton. Sporting houses were as easy to identify—Lola's, Diamond Kate, Big Mollie, Diamond Tooth Lil's, and so on. On this street a dozen dance halls employed over three hundred girls. There was night life for all, and plenty of participants, with ample reserve in the nearby hills. However there was very little trouble, as the people made their own laws and upheld them. An example was in December of 1882 when a bartender sold a drink to a minor. Instantly the town was up in arms. They gathered and destroyed his stock of liquor valued at $3,000.00.

The Denver & Rio Grande Railroad at the Rockwood Cut

The building of the D. & R. G. Railroad started northward up the Animas Canyon, a natural route, soon to be blasted out by the construction force. This closed the toll road, as much of the road was to be used for the railroad bed. The train reached Silverton July 18, 1882, over forty-five miles of one of the D. & R. G.'s most scenic routes. The first steel rails made by the Colorado Fuel and Iron Works of Pueblo went into this track at a price of $70.00 a ton. Previously, all rails had been made of iron. The pioneers thought their transportation troubles were over, but they soon learned the elements were unbeaten. Snowslides, washouts, and floods were unconquered, and there were plenty of all before too many years. However, the "Silverton" has the longest record of continuous operation of any narrow gauge railroad in the country, and does the greatest passenger business per mile of any scheduled train in the United States. Silverton's first telegraph came with the arrival of the train service.

Toll Road Between Ouray and Silverton. Present Day Million Dollar
Highway

The rich discovery of the Yankee Girl Mine in Ironton Park made
necessary a road from Ouray to Red Mountain, and Otto Mears, with his
associates, built 12 miles. About half of this was cut into solid rock walls
of the Uncompahgre Canyon. The road was then extended twelve miles
from Red Mountain into Silverton. This Ouray-Silverton road, through
the Uncompahgre Canyon and over the gorgeous Red Mountain,
constitutes Mr. Mears' most spectacular accomplishment, and still remains
the most scenic of all Colorado highways. This was the route used by the
famous Circle Route Stage for years. It was a daily service by stage coach
and horses and later by automobile. There was a toll gate at Bear Creek
Falls that operated from 1887 to 1900. A little cabin in which the
attendant stayed, was built near the creek and a big pole laid across the
bridge. When anyone drove up, he shouted for the toll keeper who came
out, lifted the pole, and collected the fee, which was $5.00 for a single
team, and $1.00 for each additional head of stock.

A water system for Silverton was built by a group of Denver and Kansas
City capitalists. The source of supply was from Boulder Creek and a five-
inch pipeline was laid from there to the present reservoir at the upper end
of Greene Street.

The Famous Grand Imperial Hotel

The Grand Hotel was the finest, and an elegant structure when built in 1883. From without it looks exactly as it did when it opened; however, the inside was restored and refurbished in 1952. Originally, it had fifty-four rooms and three baths, but today offers travelers forty rooms with bath. The beautiful mahogany bar was built for the Grand in 1882 in Denver and shipped by the railroad in sections, and the three plate glass mirrors in the back bar are the originals purchased in France. Today it again is the finest of resort hotels, and is open the year around. This is the birthplace of the famous song, "There'll be a Hot Time in the Old Town Tonight". One night a stranger was sitting in the bar when the wife of a colored porter came hurrying into the hotel lobby saying, "If I don't find that coon, there will be a hot time in this old town tonight". The words inspired the stranger and he took a piece of paper from his pocket and wrote the song. The Hub Saloon, which was located in the Grand, never closed its doors nor locked its safe except to turn on the safety catch. One night a new porter twirled the tumbler and the place had to operate on borrowed funds until a safe man could get here from Denver to open it. Jack Slattery, owner of the Hub, once hired major league baseball players to play ball in Silverton just for his entertainment.

St. Patrick's Church was organized, and in 1883 a new church building was erected. The colored people of the town purchased the old Catholic church building and had it moved to a lot on Mineral Street. This year the I.O.O.F. was instituted.

St. Patrick's Church, Erected in 1883

During the winter of 1883, mail was being carried from Silverton to Ophir on snow shoes by Swede Nilson. While he was getting ready to leave for Ophir, he kept looking at the grey sky, as it was snowing hard. His friends had tried to persuade him to wait until after the blizzard, but Swede knew how anxious the people in Ophir were to get their mail, as it was December 21—Christmas time. The postal attendant helped strap the thirty pound sack of mail on his back and was apprehensive as he watched him start off in the storm. Days passed with no word from Nilson and it was ascertained that he had never reached Ophir. At first everyone thought he had been caught in a snowslide, but when spring came, folks began to wonder. They searched the trail but he was not found that season. It was believed that there was considerable Christmas money in the mail sack and rumors circulated that the Swede had rifled the sack and skipped the country. Everyone had almost forgotten Nilson when in August 1885 he was found on the north side of the slope with the mail pack still on his back. He had been caught in a snow slide and buried under tons of snow.

In the winter of 1884, just two years after the arrival of the D. & R. G. into Silverton, a heavy storm with numerous snow slides closed the road for 77 days, from February 5th to April 22nd. Occasional mail was carried into town by volunteers, but foodstuffs not previously brought into town were done without.

The first census was taken in 1885, and showed a population of 1989 persons. At the town's crest, the population numbered 5000.

The Silverton Narrow Gauge Railroad Which Ran from Silverton to Red Mountain and Ironton Park.

Mear's Famous Turntable on Red Mountain for the Silverton Railroad.

Silverton Northern Railroad, Taps Rich Mining District.

In June, Otto Mears began the construction of the Silverton Railroad—a narrow three-foot gauge track of sixteen miles, including several switch-backs from Silverton to Red Mountain and Ironton Park. It was completed to Red Mountain in September 1889 and the Ironton stretch was completed in November, the same year. The road cost $75,000.00, at that time a large amount of money for one man to raise. This railroad made possible the shipment of low grade ores from the Red Mountain district to the Silverton Smelter for treatment. In 1889 Mears started construction of the Silverton Northern Railroad to tap the mining district north of Silverton. This line boasted a unique combination dining car and sleeper, with an extensive wine card printed in two colors and a menu whose items ranged from Porter House to Antelope cutlets. At the height of its fortunes it was one of the best money makers in the entire United States. At a time when passenger trains on main lines were grossing $1.00 a mile, the Silverton Northern four passenger runs a day were grossing $20.00 a mile, and freight trains of ore from the mines so rich that armed guards rode them all the way to the smelter in Durango. First Mears built five miles of track to Howardsville, then in 1894 he added four miles extending the line to Eureka. In 1903 he built another four miles to Animas Forks. The line to Eureka was used until the Sunnyside mine closed in 1939.

In 1889, San Juan County took advantage of the voting franchise for women and elected Nellie Tulley as the first woman treasurer of the state.

Gem Chapter Number 15, O. E. S. was organized in 1893 and in 1894 the Miners Union. In 1901, the Miners Union built their hall at an expenditure of over $35,000.00. The Union had a membership of over 1300.

Miners Union Hall, Erected in 1901.

The Silverton, Gladstone and Northerly was built in 1896 from Silverton to Gladstone to take care of the Gold King and other producing mines of the upper Cement Creek section. The train ran until about 1915, then was purchased by the Silverton Northern Railroad, and the track was later removed.

The Silverton, Gladstone and Northerly was built in 1896 to take care of The Gold King and Other Producing Mines in The Upper Cement Creek Section.

Among the ladies, there were two clubs. The Silverton Women's Club was organized by Mrs. E. G. Stoiber in April 1897 and was admitted to the State Federation the same year. The San Juan Women's Club was organized in January, 1900 and was admitted to the State Federation the same year and the General Federation the following year. The San Juan Club still functions, and has an active membership of 17.

St. John's Episcopal Church of Silverton and Christian Science Church of Silverton were organized in 1898.

The latter part of August 1901, Silverton had its first telephone communication. The Colorado Telephone Company ran its lines from Denver through Glenwood Springs, Grand Junction, Delta, Montrose, Ouray and then into Silverton. The first telephone office was upstairs in the back room of the building now known as the Recreation Hall. Phones were installed as fast as equipment would allow. The first out-of-town phone went to the Sunnyside Mine at Eureka. It was a year before the lines to Durango were in and ready for use.

In 1901 the town of Silverton purchased for $40,000.00 the water works, formerly owned by a private company. They have since expended much more for improvements. Our water is still as clear and pure as the days when the first prospector slaked his thirst from the brim of his battered hat.

The privately owned electric light system broke down during Christmas week of both the years 1901 and '02 on account of excessive demands for lights and power. The citizens voted bonds for a municipally owned utility and in 1903 the new system was in operation. This was the second alternating plant to be built in the United States. This year, Silverton also had a municipally owned sewer system which gave us the further distinction of being the first town to own all three—lights, water and sewer systems.

In 1903, the Silver Link Rebekah Lodge No. 93 was organized and the town jail, located behind the Court House, was erected.

City Jail Erected in 1903, and Now Made Into A Museum.

About noon of March 10, 1906, a snow storm started and continued for over a week. During this time, every slide in the county ran. The greatest casualty in the county was the destruction of the Shenandoah boarding and bunk house causing the death of thirteen, and injuring several others. All told, the storm took the lives of over twenty people.

City Hall, Constructed In 1907 of Dark Red Stone from the Wyman Quarry on South Mineral Creek

In 1907 the town engaged in the erection of a new City Hall at a cost of $40,000.00. The building was constructed of dark red stone from the Wyman Stone Quarry on South Mineral Creek.

The County Court House was completed in 1908 at the cost of $100,000.00, and at that time was one of the best in the state. On the court house lawn is a monument studded with samples of many ores from one hundred mine areas.

Mr. Carnegie donated the funds to build and equip our library, which is located on the corner of 10th and Reese Street.

Silverton Public Library

County Court House Taken From The Upper End of Greene Street.

The first automobile to reach Silverton came over Stony Pass on the 26th of August, 1910. It was owned and driven by Dr. D. L. Mechling of Denver. The car made the trip up the Rio Grande—the same route used by the pioneers in the '70's. Much road work had to be done as they went along. At the last steep pitch, horses had to come to the rescue and pull the car to the top of the Pass, which has an elevation of 12,500 feet. On the top of the Pass they saw two women and a man, the latter waving high the American Flag. They had walked and climbed some ten miles to be the first to greet the travelers. As they started down the Pass they were greeted every few hundred yards by people waving and shouting. They finally reached Silverton and came to a stop in front of the City Hall. Bells were ringing, the band struck up a tune, and the whole town turned out to welcome the party. The car was a thirty horsepower Croxton Keeton, a model patterned after a French Flinch by Renault, but built in United States at cost of $4,500.00. The next day, with the assistance of the county team, the car succeeded in getting to Ouray.

Mr. E. Buchanan, the County Attorney, owned the first car in Silverton, a one-cylinder 1911 Cadillac. He didn't use the car much, and the following year he sold it to Mr. Hinkley. With much sputtering and smoking, Mr. Hinkley managed to get it down Reese Street. Two years later, Mr. H. B. Maris was the owner of the second car in town, a racy little four cylinder model without a top. This was the first car to make the trip to Ouray on its own power.

Early in October, 1911 a rainy season of several weeks duration caused a flood in the Animas Canyon washing out the railroad track, bridges and even the rock railroad bed. Consequently, Silverton had a nine weeks blockade. This came before the merchants had their supplies of goods, foods, and coal for the winter. This was of course, before the days of the highways, and we depended entirely on the railroad, but Silverton again came through without any real suffering, and even had the courage and foresight to erect the present school building at this time.

Burros Loaded With Track Iron Ready To Leave Silverton

In 1913 work was started in earnest on the highway from Durango to Silverton. The first car went over this part of the highway in the fall of 1918. However, the road was not officially opened for travel until 1920. Bill Compton, Roy Roff, Fred Salfisberg, Bob Lockwood and one or two others from the power company made the trip, which was a hard one. They had to lay planks across the culverts, as there were open holes. They encountered many difficulties, but finally reached Silverton with the glory of being the first car over the road.

In 1916, the road up to the Cement Fill was being constructed. Previously, the road went up South Mineral to Chattanooga Creek then turned and went up a very steep pitch to the present highway near Johnson's Park. Usually passengers had to walk up this pitch to make the load lighter for the teams and also to give a push now and then.

The Sunnyside Mill was in operation in 1917 at Eureka. At first it handled 500 tons of ore per day, and later more units were added and 1,000 tons were put through daily, the company built and furnished a number of houses in Eureka for their employees and families. When production was at its peak, around four hundred were employed. In 1919 a terrific fire destroyed most of the buildings at the mine, and only the tram terminal and transformer house remained usable. The company rebuilt at once and mining continued on a large scale until December 1921, when they ceased operation due to the drop in the metal market. They reopened in 1922 and operated continually until 1930 in spite of a flood that washed out the railroad with no train for thirty days. They closed again until 1937 when the property reopened and operated for about eighteen months.

Eureka, Colo.—Location of the Sunnyside Mill—Now a Ghost Town

In 1918 the "flu" epidemic struck the area, with great loss of life. San Juan County probably had a greater proportion of deaths than any section of the nation. The usual percentage was about ten percent afflicted with the disease, of which about one or two percent died. Silverton suffered a loss of nine percent of our entire population within three weeks. Graves could not be dug fast enough, and it became necessary to bury in trenches. One trench contained sixty-two bodies.

The highway from Silverton to Ouray was dedicated in 1924 as the Million Dollar Highway. The dedication took place on the first large turn below the Treasury Tunnel Mine, and in 1926 a Memorial was erected at Bear Creek Falls in honor of Otto Mears, Pioneer Roadbuilder.

On March 8, 1927 the first airplane flew over Silverton. This flight was arranged by Representative E. J. Holman of San Juan County and was supposedly a "Mercy Flight" to the stricken snow bound people of Silverton as the train had been blocked for thirty-three days at this time. Letters, newspapers, and antitoxin were dropped north of town near the sub station. Helen Fleming, who still resides here, received a letter on this plane and was offered $5.00 for the envelope stamp by a stamp collector in California. She refused to sell, but her Mother sold one she had received at that time.

Then on May 24, 1932 a Travel Air six-place monoplane made a three-point landing on the Million Dollar Highway at the foot of Greene Street. The pilot, Walter Piele, brought the plane from Durango, and it was the first to land here. The pilot later lost his license for making the landing.

The last long blockade was in February 1932 and lasted ninety days. The slides came down, blocking the highways and railroad almost to Needleton. Supplies and mail were brought up the track from Needleton by mule pack train and men with toboggans freighted supplies from Ouray.

The following was taken from a Denver Post clipping of April 7, 1932: "For the first time in history of the postoffice department, it is believed, a ton of hay has been shipped by parcel post. This was revealed Wednesday in a report to the State Utilities Commission. The hay was badly needed to feed dairy cattle in the snowbound town of Silverton and was ordered by the Mullin Lumber Company of Silverton from the Farmer's Supply Company of Durango. The Durango firm was unable to ship the hay by freight because the railroad stops sixteen miles from Needleton Pass. It was decided to throw the responsibility on Uncle Sam for the delivery of the hay. The hay was pressed into bundles to conform with the maximum size and weight specified for parcel post and offered to the postmaster at Durango. The postage amounted to $14.00. When the hay had reached the end of the railroad it was transferred to Silverton by pack mule at a cost to the post office department of 5c a pound. Thus, the post office department lost $86.00 on the transaction but the cows in Silverton will munch hay for a few days at least, and the children of the isolated town will have fresh milk again."

Silverton's ore reserves have been only "scratched". This area is the most highly mineralized area in the United States, for in very few mining districts of the world are to be found the extensive variety of ores that abound in this country. Until 1893 no gold in the ore was paid for except when it was plainly visible to the naked eye or made a good showing in the pan. In the Sunnyside extension several hundred thousand dollars were taken out in free gold. Kendall Mountain and Silver Lake Basin have been the center of free gold discoveries at intervals since 1872. The first free gold in the country was taken from the Little Giant lode, three sacks of which were reported to have been worth $4,000 to $5,000. This was in 1872. In 1905 and '06 the Old Hundred Mine produced considerable free gold, taking from $30,000 to $40,000 off the plates each month in a forty stamp mill.

Many of the mines used aerial trams to transport the ore over the surface to the mills and railroads. Among some of the larger trams are: Gold Prince, 13,000 feet; Sunnyside, 15,600 feet; Kittemac, 10,000 feet; Iowa Tiger, 14,375 feet; Silver Lake, 13,730 feet; Mogul, 10,000 feet; and Shenandoah, 10,000 feet.

Divided into forty prominent gulches, each one a fair sized mining district in itself, the county displays a vast network of big veins of low grade ore in addition to the occasional rich strikes. San Juan is the center of a mineral empire, with ore, coal, timber, water and power. It needs business men, builders of enterprise, to make fortunes for themselves and to bring out the great wealth that still lies in the mountains. The decline in mining activity in the county has been due primarily to the decline in metal prices—not shortage of ore.

Since the earliest records were kept, the county, through 1957, has produced $138,218,339 in gold, silver, copper, lead and zinc. Gold has led the values in this county with a total of thirty-nine and a half million dollars; lead was a close second with over thirty-six million; silver third, with over thirty and a half million. Copper totaled $12,353,827, and zinc $19,406,616.

There are seven "Ghost Towns" in the immediate area; Howardsville, five miles northeast, is the location of the first court house. There were numerous buildings here including a post office and school, many of which still stand. Middleton, located in the 1890's is two miles above

Howardsville. It also had a postoffice and school and is the site of the Nugget and Kittemac Mines. Eureka, established in the 1870's, became a ghost town in 1938. As I have previously mentioned, this was the site of the Sunnyside Mine and there were over six hundred inhabitants. One of the few remaining buildings you will see is the old town hall and fire house.

A few miles farther up the Animas River Canyon is Animas Forks, which was one of the busiest mining centers. The railroad served this place and the big activity was at the Gold Prince Mill. Animas Forks also supported a number of thriving businesses, including a fine newspaper, school and post office. The big attraction here today is the old jail, built entirely of 2 × 6's and hand-forged window bars. The townsite was laid out in the late 1870's and was deserted by 1923.

At the head of the Animas is Mineral Point. It was an important stage stop for the Silverton to Ouray stage coaches as this road was used while the present Million Dollar Highway was under construction. They boasted of having the highest post office in the United States. There is probably no area in the county where outcrops are so numerous and lodes and veins are so conspicuous, as in the area immediately surrounding Mineral Point. The summit of Mineral Point is formed of a heavy vein of nearly solid white quartz sixty feet wide.

Old Jail Built of 2 × 6's and Hand Forged Window Bars. Still Standing in Animas Forks Which Is Now A Ghost Town.

Filming A Movie On Blair Street

Gladstone, located nine miles north of Silverton on Cement Creek, had a population of around 2000, and has now been a ghost town for probably thirty years. Chattanooga is northwest of Silverton on the Silverton to Ouray highway, established in 1878, and served by the Silverton Railroad—sometimes called the Red Mountain Railroad. The last school taught there was in 1902.

Silverton remains unspoiled. Here, unbelievably preserved, you can live today in the romantic atmosphere of old, for it is as it was at the turn of the century.

So perfect is the atmosphere of the town, particularly Blair Street with its two blocks of the original sporting houses and gambling dives, that film companies have used it numerous times.

Setting The Scene For A "Take" On Blair Street.

Since the first, Silverton has run the gamut of hope and prosperity. Around it boom towns turned into ghost towns, but Silverton has gone on almost unchanged. The silver panic of 1893 and the national panic of 1907 wiped out many mining towns, but Silverton has become known as, "A Mining Camp that Never Quits".

TRAIN SAVED ON I.C.C. DECISION

These were the headlines in the Silverton Standard, Silverton's weekly newspaper on Friday, May 4th, 1962. The following is a copy of the article:

The long awaited decision by the Interstate Commerce Commission, Washington D. C., was handed down Wednesday morning and assures continuation of the Narrow Gauge Line from Durango to Silverton for an undetermined time.

A telegram from Senator John Carroll and Congressman Wayne Aspinall was received by the Silverton Standard early Wednesday morning, and read as follows:

"Happy to inform you Interstate Commerce Commission this morning issued decision refusing to permit abandonment by Rio Grande Railroad of narrow gauge railway connecting Durango and Silverton. This preserves status of line as a common carrier."

While Silverton people were quite sure such a decision would be forthcoming it is gratifying to know that the action of the commission was final and in our favor.

The narrow gauge line has been operating into Silverton since 1882 and is at present one of the last and oldest regularly scheduled passenger lines in the United States operating on a three-foot track.

Business over the line has been growing steadily for twelve years. Last year the passenger figure hit near the 40,000 mark and an increase is noted annually.

"Christ of The Mines Shrine", Overlooking The Town From Anvil Mountain, Stands As A Symbol Of Faith.

This beautiful structure is 12 feet in height and was hand-carved in Italy out of Carrara Marble. Erected in 1959, the background niche is 24 feet high and spreads 40 feet along the mountainside.